Raintree is an imprint of Capstone Global Library Limited, a company incorporated in England and Wales having its registered office at 264 Banbury Road, Oxford, OX2 7DY – Registered company number: 6695582

www.raintree.co.uk
myorders@raintree.co.uk

Text © Capstone Global Library Limited 2019
The moral rights of the proprietor have been asserted

Edited by Clare Lewis and Helen Cox Cannons
Designed by Dynamo
Original illustrations © Capstone Global Library Limited 2019
Picture research by Dynamo
Production by Tori Abraham
Originated by Capstone Global Library Limited
Printed and bound in India

ISBN 978 1 4747 7306 5
22 21 20 19
10 9 8 7 6 5 4 3 2 1

British Library Cataloguing in Publication Data
A full catalogue record for this book is available from the British Library.

Acknowledgements
We would like to thank the following for permission to reproduce photographs:
Getty Images: E+/123ducu, 23, E+/Dean Mitchell, 24, E+/Johnny Greig, 12-13, E+/kali9, 18, E+/kate_sept2004, 20-21, E+/M_a_y_a, 11, E+/miodrag ignjatovic, 7, E+/wundervisuals, 17, iStock Editorial/stu99, 27, iStock/Daisy-Daisy, 9, iStock/DisobeyArt, 25, iStock/DragonImages, Cover, 1, iStock/Marc Bruxelle, 26, iStock/monkeybusinessimages, 28, iStock/Rostislav_Sedlacek, 14-15, iStock/Sinenkiy, 6, iStock/sswartz, 4-5, iStock/Steve Debenport, 8, istock/svetikd, 21 Bottom Right, iStock/Wavebreak, 5, iStock/XiXinXing, 15 Bottom Right.

We would like to thank Sam MIlls from Stonewall and Charlotte Mitchell for their invaluable help with the preparation of this book.

Contents

I'm Ali! Look out for our helpful tips throughout the book.

Hi! I'm Annie and this is my dog, Charlie.

Some words are shown in bold, **like this**. You can find out what they mean by looking in the glossary.

What is gender?

When a baby is born, a doctor looks at the baby's body parts and gives it a **sex**, male or female. If you are male, the doctor says you are a boy. If you are female, the doctor says you are a girl. This is your **gender.** For a small number of babies, it can be hard to tell their sex. If this happens, the child is sometimes called intersex, Their gender is still usually described as a boy or a girl.

▲ The first thing many parents want to find out about their new baby is whether it is a girl or a boy.

Most people expect certain things about the new baby depending on whether it has been described as a girl or a boy.

Gender stereotypes

Many people have particular ideas about what girls should be like and what boys should be like. These ideas are gender **stereotypes**. A stereotype is a set idea about a person or a group that is quite often wrong. One stereotype is that all girls like pink and boys like blue. While some girls do like pink, others do not. And not all boys like blue!

The colours you like are up to you!

Often, boys are given trucks to play with and not dolls. This is an example of stereotyping.

It's not just about colours. Stereotypes affect many things, like the clothes we wear, interests we have or toys we play with. Some people decide what we are like because of stereotypes. But stereotypes are not always true.

How you feel

Being a boy or a girl is about how you feel, not just what your body is like. It is also about how you **express**, or show, yourself to the rest of the world.

TIP

Remember, clothes and toys are just clothes and toys - they don't have genders!

It might take a long time to work out who you are. That's OK. Everyone is different.

You might have lots of different feelings about yourself. You might like some of the **traditional** ideas of being a girl or a boy, but not all of them. This is OK. It's normal for people to have mixed feelings.

Being transgender

How you feel about your gender is called your **gender identity**. Most people don't think about the gender they were given at birth very often. This is because it matches their gender identity. But some people's feelings about their own gender don't match the **sex** and **gender** the doctor gave them when they were born.

A boy can feel more like a girl, or a girl can feel more like a boy. These people describe themselves as **transgender**, or trans.

Transgender people might feel uncomfortable with being called a boy or a girl. They might feel like they aren't a boy or a girl. Sometimes these people use the word **non-binary** to describe their gender.

When you were young, you probably didn't think about how you feel about gender very much. As you get older, you might find you have questions.

People who are transgender cannot change the way their brains and their feelings work. It is not a choice. But they can change how they look so that it matches how they feel. They can wear the clothes and hairstyles that they want.

Transgender people can even change the way they move or speak. They can also ask people to describe them as "he", "she" or "they" to match how they feel about their gender.

TIP

If you think the way you feel doesn't match your gender, don't be scared. Try to talk about it with a trusted adult. Remember, you're not alone.

◀ These women were born male but now dress as women.

Some people feel very strongly that the sex or gender they were given when they were born doesn't match their gender identity. They might even feel uncomfortable in their body, because it doesn't look the way they feel inside.

It is really important for these people to speak to someone they trust. Sometimes it is a good idea to talk to a doctor, who can give more information on different ways to help.

▶ Some people may talk about their feelings about gender with a doctor.

Everyone is different. Some people know from a young age that their gender and their gender identity don't match. Others take longer to understand how they feel. There is no time limit.

▲ Whatever you are going through, talk to friends or someone else you trust.

Be kind

If you know someone who is transgender, try to be **understanding**. They might seem different from you or from many other people but we are all different in lots of ways. You should never tease or bully anyone for being different in any way.

Many people think that girls should dress in one way and boys in another. But there is no real reason for this. Anyone should feel free to wear dresses or trousers. It is up to them!

TIP

Make sure that you talk about transgender people in the right way. If the person feels like a girl and wants to be known as a girl, use "she" and "her", even if she was labelled a boy at birth.

▲ Be a good friend. Listen to people if they want to talk.

Same-sex couples

There are lots of ways that families can be different. Perhaps you live with just your dad? Maybe you live with your grandparents? Perhaps you have two mums, or two dads?

When someone is in a relationship with someone of the same sex, we describe them as a same-sex couple. Even though some families are more unusual, there is no wrong kind of family.

Sometimes having same-sex parents can be difficult. While you might be used to it, what other people say may bother you. **Prejudice** is when people have unfair opinions about those who are different from them.

TIP

Try talking to your parents or carers about same-sex relationships. It may help you to understand more about them or cope with any prejudice.

◀ Same-sex couples may decide to raise children together.

How to deal with difference

Seeing other people in a same-sex relationship might be confusing. If it's something you are not used to, you may have questions. Just remember that everybody has feelings. They might be different from yours or those of your family but that's OK. It is important to be kind and **respect** their differences.

TIP

By asking questions you learn more about the things you don't understand. But first make sure people are happy to talk to you about their relationships.

If you have questions about same-sex relationships, it might help you to write them down.

Share your feelings

Some people are more understanding of difference than others. Transgender people are sometimes bullied because of who they are. People in same-sex relationships can also face prejudice.

Your parents or carers might not understand your feelings. Try to explain to them how you feel.

Everyone has a right to happiness and to love who they choose.

If you are being bullied, it might make you feel sad or angry. Talk to your parents or carers, or another adult you trust. If you'd rather not talk to them, ask them to help you find someone you do feel happy to talk to.

Togetherness

Some people who don't fit gender stereotypes work together to help other people understand. They have made a symbol of togetherness. The colours of the rainbow flag stand for all the different types of people in the world. The flag also lets people know that no one should be forced to fit in with gender stereotypes.

TIP

There are lots of different ways to be a girl or to be a boy! No one should have to do things or feel a certain way just because they were born a boy or a girl.

Families come together to celebrate differences.

Celebrating gender differences

People are not all the same. If your family is different from your friends' families, celebrate that! Always feel proud of who you and your friends are!

▲ It is OK to be different. Be yourself!

Ali and Annie's advice

- It is OK to look and feel different from your friends. Differences are what makes us interesting!

- Be proud of who you are and the people in your family.

- Accept others for who they are. Everyone deserves respect.

- Don't cover up your feelings. It doesn't make them go away.

- Talk to a trusted adult if you are worried about anything.

- Ask questions if there are things you don't understand.

- If you face prejudice, ask an adult for help.

- Celebrate your differences!

Glossary

express say or show how you feel about yourself to other people

gender whether you are called a girl or a boy

gender identity the way you feel about your gender

non-binary when a person does not feel like a boy or a girl

prejudice unfair treatment of people who are different from most other people

respect having a good opinion about someone and showing them that you care about their feelings by treating them well

sex male or female

stereotype widely held but simple idea about how a person or group is or behaves

traditional beliefs and ways of doing things that have lasted a long time without changing

transgender when the way someone feels about their gender doesn't match the gender, or sex, that a doctor gave them when they were born

understanding to be aware of other people's feelings and treat them with respect and kindness, even if they are different to you

Find out more

Books

A House for Everyone, Jo Hirst (Jessica Kingsley Publishers, 2018)

Who Am I? I Am Me!, Jayneen Sanders (Educate2Empower Publishing, 2018)

Who Are You?: The Kids' Guide to Gender Identity, Brook Pessin-Whedbee (Jessica Kingsley Publishers, 2016)

Website

www.childline.org.uk/info-advice

If you want help about anything, from bullying to family life, visit the Childline website.